GOD'S
GAME PLAN

SCRIPTURE INDEX INCLUDED

RICHARD A. HASLER

C.S.S. Publishing Co., Inc.

Lima, Ohio

GOD'S GAME PLAN: SPORTS ANECDOTES
FOR PREACHING AND OTHER PROCLAIMERS OF THE WORD

Library of Congress Cataloging-in-Publication Data

Hasler, Richard A.
    God's game plan: sports anecdotes for preaching and other proclaimers of the word / by Richard A. Hasler.
        p.   cm.
    ISBN 1-55673-206-6
    1. Homiletical illustrations.   2. Sports—Anecdotes.   I. Title.
BV4225.2.H36   1990
251'.08--dc20   89-25165
                                                                        CIP

9023 / ISBN 1-55673-206-6

To our son, Rick
versatile athlete
and
physical fitness professional

Contents

Introduction

"Whoever wants to know the heart and mind of America had better learn baseball." The oft-quoted statement of Columbia University Professor Jacques Barzun is an underlying assumption of the following collection of sports anecdotes for preaching.

I have detected in my own preaching, in college teaching and in writing, that baseball and other sports provide valuable metaphors for illuminating the Christian gospel. This anthology has been compiled for Christian communicators including pastors, teachers, counselors, writers and other leaders. The preaching task in particular, requires stories and examples to illustrate basic Christian truths. The sports anecdotes in the collection are designed to add color, warmth, humor and imagination to the preacher's message.

Of course, such an approach is not new. The Apostle Paul and other New Testament writers employed athletic images to express the view that the Christian life was a contest, a challenge and a struggle. (See the appendix for specific references.) We are not certain that Paul had a box seat at the Isthmian Games near Corinth, nor, can we be sure that he was an avid reader of the sports pages of the Corinthian *Times*. Whatever his sources were, however, he was conversant with the athletic image, which he adroitly applied to the arena of faith.

My own keen interest in sports dates back to my youth. Although active in many sports, my great passion was baseball. I played baseball in high school and with American Legion teams in the summer. I even had a brief stint as a catcher in professional minor league baseball before going to college. David Halberstam in his book *Summer of '49,* recounts the fantastic pennant race between the New York Yankees and the Boston Red Sox. During that same summer I was having the time of my life as a teenager playing in the lowly minors and dreaming of even greater things to come.

Later, when I began theological studies at Princeton, I became acquainted with superior athletes who demonstrated for me that it was possible to combine a love of sports with a strong Christian commitment. Among these models were Donn Moomaw, first team All-American linebacker from UCLA, a classmate, and Richard Armstrong, former public relations director of the Baltimore Orioles, both classmates.

7

Thereafter began my fascination to search for connecting links between sports and Biblical faith. The stories I have made the most of in my preaching have ranged from the simplicity of the Charlie Brown cartoons with his sincere but losing baseball team to the more sophisticated wit of Marriane Moore, a poet and a critic. Moore, incidentally, revived her interest in baseball late in life when one day she was taken to a Brooklyn Dodger game and was held spellbound by what she called the "vim" with which catcher Roy Campanella played the game.

In more recent years as the organizing pastor of Pioneer Presbyterian Church, a new church development of the Presbytery of Muskingum Valley in eastern Ohio, I have re-discovered the effectiveness of the sports analogy in preaching. In a brand new congregation consisting of people with a wide variety of church backgrounds, and in some cases no church background at all, I have found sports to be a common denominator that binds us together. Furthermore, with so many walkers and joggers in the congregation and others who take physical fitness seriously, a message that blends emphases upon the body, mind and the spirit usually elicits a positive response.

From my extensive reading I have gathered sports anecdotes from writers who have availed themselves of such stories and examples in their own interpretation of the Christian faith. These illustrations cover the whole range of sports from team sports (baseball, football, basketball) to individual sports (track and field, golf, skiing). Famous athletes and coaches appear in the selections, such as Roger Bannister, Lou Gehrig, Bobby Jones, Eric Liddell, Jackie Robinson, Jim Ryun, Bud Wilkinson and John Wooden. Other selections mirror more common experiences in and observations upon sports.

The selections which follow are arranged according to ten topics that combine both the athletic image and the Christian life.

1. Contending — The call to Christian discipleship is not to be an idle spectator but to play with vigor and enthusiasm in the game of life.

2. Training — The athlete of Christ develops self-control, learns basic habits and knows the rules of the game.

3. Risking — As in sports, so in the Christian life risk-taking sets apart the dilettante from the fully committed participant.

4. Motivating — Individuals cannot do well in the race of faith without motivation and encouragement from others within the Christian community.

5. Playing — At the heart of loving and serving God is a playful spirit, a sense of joy and of celebration.

6. Persevering — Sooner or later in the arena, pressures build to the point that we are tempted to quit, but those who eventually overcome call upon deep spiritual reserves to enable them to press on to the end.

7. Projecting — Keeping our eyes on the primary goal, namely the prize of Christ, assures us that we are moving in the right direction.

8. Losing — All those who engage in a contest, athletic or spiritual, sooner or later will taste defeat; the all-important question is how we respond to losing.

9. Winning — We all long for victories in our lives, but we also need to probe deeply to be sure we know what it really means to win.

10. Witnessing — Ultimately, what matters at the close of the race is the kind of story we tell, the type of witness we make for our Lord.

A caveat should be inserted here to remind us that the athletic image is only one of many metaphors to describe the Christian life. Sports imagery should not be absolutized as the only image or even the best image. Further, sports should not be thought of as a religion in itself, something it has virtually become in the minds of some of its devotees. Nonetheless, the athletic image remains a powerful symbol with which to make connections between the contemporary world and the inner life of the faith adventurer.

Believing that many men and women within our sports-conscious society will relate to Christian insights couched in sports analogies, I enthusiastically share these anecdotes with all who seek to interpret more effectively the Good News in our day.

I am grateful to the following people who have assisted me in one way or another: Editorial Director Dawn Lausa who has been very helpful in preparing the manuscript for publication; Carolyn Henry who efficiently typed the manuscript's final draft; Librarians Ellen Mumma (Belpre Public), Barbara Boyce (Trinity Seminary,

9

Columbus) and Joel R. Bowman (Union Seminary, Richmond) who supplied books not available in my own library; Presbytery leaders including Executive Presbyters Philip Bembower (who initiated our mission project), the late Fronda Lyon (Interim), Henry Snedeker Meier (Associate) and Hugh Berry (who superbly guided our young congregation through its building phase) and esteemed mentors Dr. Roland Fredericks and his wife, Margaret; the marvelous and adventurous people of Pioneer Presbyterian Church, Belpre, Ohio, with whom I shared most of these stories in Sunday worship; our children, Rick and Karen and their families, especially grandson, Michael, an ardent Cleveland Indian fan and finally, my wife, Arlene, enthusiastic partner in this mission venture, whose radiant, life-affirming attitude encourages me and to whom I am indebted most of all.

1 — CONTENDING

Born to Play This Game

During the 1980 Olympics, almost everyone expected that the Russian ice hockey team would defeat the United States team. Russia had won game after game against some of the finest professional teams in the world, and the amateurs from the United States didn't seem to have a chance. The only thing uncertain was how big the Russian win would be. The United States' victory is recalled by many as one of the most exciting in American sports history. But most people don't know the words spoken to the United States team by Coach Herb Brooks just before the game — maybe one of the best pep talks in history. He simply said, "Gentlemen, you were born to play this game!"

The God who is in charge has said something similar to us: "You were born to praise Me. Do it well, because this is your function in the world."

Stephen Brown
If God Is In Charge . . .
Page 138[1]

Agony

The Greek word translated *race* is *agon*, from which we get our word agony. It signifies a wrestling match or race where endurance and determination must overcome the aching desire to quit. In a race, such as the quarter mile, there are moments toward the end when the body cries out to let up. Pain starts in the calf and works up through the hamstrings to the gluteus maximus. At times it is so intense it feels like a burning fire. Agony is the best way to describe it. A wrestler knows the same pain when struggling against a powerful opponent who seeks to crush him to the mat by sheer weight and relentless hold. It would be so easy to let up and let a fall be declared, but the champion heart fights through, waiting for that opportunistic moment of lost concentration or of a shifting of weight that allows an explosive hold-breaking surge.

Paul describes his efforts to bring others to their full maturity as the agonizing of an athlete . . .

Louis H. Evans, Jr.
Hebrews, The Communicator's Commentary
Page 218[2]

The Demand

When I was a boy, the little fellows of my age played a kind of softball down on the lower part of the playing field while the big boys played on the big diamond. My sister had a boyfriend who was playing on the big diamond, and I said to one of my chums, "I bet you the next time Willy Williams comes to bat, he'll let me take his place!" So we went up to where they were, and I asked Willy. Of course he knew better than to refuse — when his turn came, he let me take it. What happened I shall never forget. Though I was frightened and could hardly manage the heavy bat, the pitcher threw the ball as hard to me as he did to the big boys. When I turned away after three strikes, there was so much more to me than there had been before. The demand had summoned my fragments into a moment of focus that has influenced me down to the present time.

Howard Thurman
Disciplines of the Spirit
Page 31[3]

The Great Association of Onlookers

We suffer today from a spectator complex — watching, but doing nothing. We see a play and we are deeply disturbed; we weep a little, clench our fists at the wrong or the injustice walking the stage — and then go home and forget it! We feel without acting.

Let's put it in the church. On the gridiron of life, the church is playing its game against stubborn opposition — against the well-coached teams of low public mores, materialism and selfishness. In the stands sit the non-churchmen, criticizing the churchmen, giving a Bronx cheer when the church is thrown for a loss, yet never offering to put on a suit and shoulder pads and get into the game, never offering to help the team of God on the field. They belong to the great Association of Onlookers, those who talk and shout but will not work. Theirs is a comprehension without ensuing change.

Louis H. Evans
Make Your Faith Work
Pages 40-41[4]

Do You Really Want to Dive?

I remember the time my mother taught me to dive. One morning in April when the sun had barely begun to warm the water, she brought me to the local YWCA for my very first dive. No one was by the pool at that hour but a sleepy lifeguard and some overly zealous sunbathers.

I put my arms over my ears and bent my knees as mom had taught me that winter. Eyes screwed shut, I concentrated as hard as I could to make my legs push off from the wall. Finally, still in position, I opened my eyes and looked at my mother. "I can't."

The lifeguard broke in from across the pool, "Maybe you should wait until she's a few years older."

"She's big enough now," Mom returned. To me she said, "If you wait until the water's perfectly warm or until you're perfectly ready, you'll be waiting forever. You've got a chance now. Do you really want to dive?"

"I want to dive, mom."

"Good! I know you can."

I crouched back into position and took a deep breath. "Tuck your head more," advised mom. I tucked, and, with painful effort, forced my legs to throw my body off the wall, head-first into the cold water. I never felt the shock of it in the exhilaration of being able to dive. I surfaced to sunshine and the sound of the lifeguard's good-natured applause.

Leslie Bush
"A Diving Lesson"
New Catholic World
March-April 1985
Page 77[5]

The Doer Makes Mistakes

Why not call the first time-out? First among several factors is condition. I have always told my teams that we are going to be in better condition than the other team and we want our opponents to need time-outs for a rest. I don't say I think we are going to be in better condition or we are going to try to be. I say we are going to be in better condition, a positive statement.

Being in better condition pays dividends if you can put the pressure on an opponent and keep it on, both offensively and defensively. This does not necessarily have to be done with a pressing defense. A tight pressure defense may serve the same purpose, providing, of course, that we are constantly and continuously applying offensive pressure also. I constantly repeat the admonition I learned from Piggy Lambert at Purdue: "The team that makes the most mistakes will probably win." There is much truth in that statement if you analyze it properly. The doer makes mistakes, and *I want doers on my team* — players who make things happen.

John Wooden (as told to Jack Tobin)
They Call Me Coach
Page 136[6]

Wrestling

"It's a strange feeling," he said as he prayed, "wrestling with the one I'm trying to love." Others agreed. You could hear it under their breaths. He had struck a chord. By the one he loved he meant God, not his wife. He is an executive of a large corporation. He is responsible for many people.

I have heard him pray like this before. His prayers are always short and labored. He falters, as he rarely does in business. I have an idea such faltering is good for him. He is getting in touch with a lost part of himself. It is getting in touch with him.

He calls it wrestling. That's all right, of course, because it's manly. But unbeknownst to him, there's more to it than that. It goes all the way back. Jacob wrestled with God on the banks of the River Jabbok. My friend is a modern Jacob. The story is as old as it is new. It is the age-old story of trying to find peace with God.

I have an idea such peace is on its way for my friend. It is coming through his struggle. His struggle is the submerged part of himself emerging. God is coming into view. Prayer is letting God emerge . . .

Robert K. Hudnut
This People, This Parish
Page 79[7]

17

2 — TRAINING

Exercising Self-control

When the Olympics were held in Mexico City, there was a young swimmer who had hopes of winning several gold medals. He failed to live up to his high expectations. So he went home and began a more intensive training program than he ever thought was possible. When the contests were held in Munich in 1972, the whole world was thrilled by the unbelievable series of record-breaking swimming events won by Mark Spitz, who went home with more gold medals than any individual had ever won in Olympic competition. It was the same young man!

There has probably never been a lesson pounded home with such force as this: You cannot excel in sports unless you exercise self-control in order to put your body in first-class physical condition. Every coach tries to instill this thought in the minds of the athletes he works with. He can set rules about getting enough sleep and the proper diet, but a coach cannot possibly oversee every minute of a person's life. Any would-be-athlete has to exercise self-control and cannot depend on the coach to supervise every detail of his life. Yet in spite of what should be common knowledge to all of us, there are great numbers of athletes who operate on the assumption that they will somehow be the one and only exception to that rule.

Orien Johnson
Becoming Transformed
Page 73[1]

18

Blocking and Tackling

If you and I want the coming year to be marked by a real newness within, we would do well to review some of the ancient practices which good people have found helpful over the centuries. I pastored in Green Bay, Wisconsin, during part of the period that Vince Lombardi was coaching the Packers to football immortality. Mr. Lombardi was often asked about trick plays and the secrets of coaching; he always answered that it was simply a matter of blocking and tackling. There were no new, clever ideas that really mattered unless one mastered the fundamentals of the game.

I've concluded that the same is true of the spiritual life. Books, retreats, and religious conferences are constantly promising us some new formula for spiritual vitality. Some of them may stimulate us for a time. But, in the end, we'll need to come back to "blocking and tackling" — such basic matters as Bible reading, prayer, group worship and sharing, and good devotional reading.

Sunday School

> J. Ellsworth Kalas
> **Reading the Signs**
> Page 48[2]

Self-limitation

I am reminded of a coach who places restraints on his players' activities to keep them healthy and properly conditioned for the coming game. A basketball player, for example, will be restrained by his coach from playing sandlot football during basketball season, not because his coach doesn't want him to have physical exercise, but because he wants to keep him healthy so that he can enjoy basketball to the fullest without a sandlot injury . . .

Likewise, when we repent and ask forgiveness, we are admitting that a part of our lives has lost its way in confusion, and we now turn toward the Lord of new beginnings for help and restoration. Self-limitation admits that each of the powerful possibilities of my life need discipline in order to achieve their fulfillment.

Earl Palmer
The 24-Hour Christian
Page 88[3]

Finding the Goalposts

In life, as in aviation and in sports, there are many stories of "Wrong-Way Corrigans," who like the fabled aviator, took off in the wrong direction! Or like the football hero who ran the wrong way because he didn't know where the goalposts were! Unlike him they are not addled by a blow on the head, but by a blow in the mind. The loss of moral and spiritual goalposts in our world today is another tragic absurdity resulting from man's loss of a living faith in God.

For faith in God is the willingness to act on the conviction that there are goalposts in the game of life; that is that there is a moral order in our human existence that, when accepted and obeyed, gives meaning and direction to our living.

Lance Webb
On the Edge of the Absurd
Page 94[4]

How Words Are Used And Abused

St. Augustine once described himself as a vendor of words. I suppose preachers could describe themselves as vendors of words. We live by speaking. The uttering of words is a very important part of our vocation. So, early in my ministry I decided that if I was going to live by speaking, then every year I would read or reread a book of grammar to remind me of how words are used and abused.

I wish that more people who live by words would read books of grammar. I wish, for example, that some of our sports commentators would do so. Have you ever noticed that in football there is never a third down. There is a third-down situation. Not long ago, in a game I watched, we encountered a measurement situation. I am not sure how that differs from a measurement, but nowadays everything is a situation. And then there is Howard Cosell, whom I admire very much. During the Olympics he said that "one boxer threw more punches in terms of number." If you are going to throw more punches, that's the way to do it!

R. Maurice Boyd
A Lover's Quarrel with the World
Page 25[5]

The Quick Release

Life isn't all "Chariots of Fire" and Christmas mornings. There are Februarys and Marches and Junes and Septembers. Some tragedies almost knock us out of the apple tree. There are accidents and illnesses, and family breakups, and hillside stranglers and storms. We do our best to cope — to manage these adverse circumstances. But at some point we have to yield ultimate control of the outcome. We have to rediscover the secret of *release.*

Part of being a Christian is letting go. Football passers have to master the quick release, and we must learn to release our grip on a lot of things, including material possessions.

James W. Angell
Accept No Imitations
Page 121[6]

Turn Your Other Cheek

I think of Jackie Robinson and the real service he provided to millions of people — players and fans alike — when he broke a long standing barrier and opened the big leagues to black athletes. As Branch Rickey, owner of the Brooklyn Dodgers, prepared Robinson to sign a contract, he wondered if the young player would be equal to the challenge. Would Robinson be able to stay out of fights, both on and off the field? Could he behave in such a way that he would neither arouse black fans nor openly antagonize white fans? Obviously, Robinson was going to need to be more than just a great player of baseball.

One day, Rickey called Robinson into his office and showed him a copy of Giovanni Papini's book, *The Life of Christ*. Then he quoted these words: "Ye have heard that it hath been said, An eye for an eye, and a tooth for a tooth; But I say unto you, that ye resist not evil: But whosoever shall smite thee on the right cheek, turn to him the other also."

"Now," Rickey said softly to Robinson, "can you do it? You will have to promise that for the first three years in baseball, you will turn your other cheek. I know you are naturally combative. But for three years — three years — you will have to do it the only way it can be done. Three years — can you do it?" Robinson was a devout Christian, but he was going to pay a high price — both for himself and as a service to generations of athletes who would walk the path that he had opened.

John Thomas Randolph
The Best Gift
Pages 70-71[7]

Shoving One Another

Before our son's freshman football game last Saturday, one of his coaches shouted at a player and abruptly dismissed him from the field. A coach on the sidelines looked squarely through the bars of the boy's helmet, spoke sternly to him, and sent him to the locker room. We wondered what could have ever evoked such a strong response from the coaches. As soon as Matthew got home from the game, we asked him. He answered simply: "He shoved his teammate."

What a profound principle: If you are in it to win, you work together to defeat the opponent. Shoving your own threatens the effort.

For a long time I have felt that we Christians have afforded ourselves a debilitating luxury, that of brother bashings. In particular, we tend to shove our leaders.

Most pastors, teachers, missionaries, elders, and national spokesmen understand that unwarranted criticism, innuendo, misunderstanding, and maligning of motives go with the territory of leadership. But it doesn't make it right. The rest of us must recognize our responsibility to hold up such leaders and make sure we don't waste time shoving one another while the adversary wins the day.

Joseph M. Stowell
"The Only Good Fight"
Moody Monthly
October 1988
Page 4[8]

The Rules of the Game

If a visitor from another planet were to drop to earth on New Year's Day and find himself in front of a color television set watching football games back to back, he would probably not know what to make of this. Try to imagine what it would be like to see this for the first time: great hulking humans, dressed for combat, rushing, kicking, tackling, pulling, charging, smashing. And all this violence to get a little leather ball through some poles at the end of the field! If our interplanetary visitor were a sensitive being he would probably be shocked and cry out to stop the violence.

But we explain to him that this is what we call a game . . .

We have learned to fight . . . on football fields. Can we learn to fight in church? It appears to me that, when we know the name of the game, the rules of the game and learn to play fair according to the rules, we can tolerate very high levels of conflict.

James D. Glasse
Putting It Together in the Parish
Pages 113, 116[9]

One More Downhill Run

My father taught me to ski when I was a young boy. I recall one of his first pieces of advice on the slope: "Remember, son, that more accidents happen in the final hour of the day than at any other time." I now know that he was correct.

Trying to get one more downhill run in before the ski tow closes, some skiers will rush down the slope forgetting that their bodies are tired and that their reflexes are no longer sharp. Shadows are long; icy and bare spots are hidden. The combination of a depleted body and obstacles not easily seen creates conditions (environments, if you please) in which accidents are far more likely to happen.

My dad was right; at the end of the day one should ski much more cautiously because the good skier knows himself and he doesn't trust the terrain.

Many men and women trying to follow the Lord make their world-breaking choices in similar times of extreme fatigue. Again, not necessarily the physical fatigue after a long day's work; but the fatigue of the spirit and the emotions that occurs after the lengthy period of time when frustration and difficulties have increased to an intense pitch.

Gordon MacDonald
Rebuilding Your Broken World
Pages 120-121[10]

3 — RISKING

Maximizing Opportunities

A few months ago, I gave the invocation at a banquet where the venerated Wayne Woodrow Hayes, longtime coach of the Ohio State Buckeyes, was the speaker. Halfway through his address, Woody took off on the evils of the forward pass. He explained the horror of trajectory. That's what happens to the ball between the passer and the receiver. If it's perfect, the consequence is a completion. If not, two of the three possible effects of throwing a pass result: an incompletion or, perish the thought, an interception.

Woody explained why some defensive backs get more interceptions than others. It's a matter of courage and position. As soon as the quarterback drops back to pass, the tension is on. The defensive back has two choices. He can play it safe and simply stay far behind the receiver so as to make the tackle after the catch. Or, he can do the job right and position himself so as to appropriately step between the receiver and the ball at precisely the right moment.

The first choice minimizes risk.

The second maximizes opportunity.

Which one the player chooses depends on the degree of his security. In my opinion, this is also the difference between All-Americans and also-rans. The All-American believes in himself, and not fearing failure in pursuit of excellence, he'll opt for courage and position every time.

The same principle applies to using the gifts God has given us. We can bury them and stay the same, or risk and grow.

Barry L. Johnson
Choosing Hope
Pages 84-85[1]

The Jump That Really Counted

As a youngster, I in my boyish imagination was filled with dreams of athletic prowess. These dreams were nourished by visits to the track meets at neighboring Cornell University. There the pole-vaulter took the center of my stage. He posed with his long pole pointed diagonally in front of him, and then pounded down the runway, set the pole in the prepare socket, and went soaring high into the air over the bar.

Full of enthusiasm, I would return home and set up my own bar in the backyard. Then I would get a long pole, take a studied pose, pound down the sidewalk into the backyard as if in full view of a grandstand, set my pole in the socket and . . . well . . . that was about as far as I ever got.

This didn't bother me too much, though, because I had seen athletes soar over the bar. I knew that it had been done, and even when my muscular efforts were at an end I imagined myself soaring over the bar. No one could tell *me* that I hadn't gone over the bar! To an onlooker, my form up to the point of the jump must have seemed marvelous, but I guess in retrospect that it was the jump that really counted.

I have often reflected upon that experience. Protestant Christians are much like that youngster. They have inherited a style of life, which dares to take the jump of faith into the world of the morrow. They have patterned themselves after heroic models, posing as men of prayer . . . patterning themselves after Christ . . . And they have accepted this pose as descriptive of their life's actions for so long that they have really begun to believe it all.

Henry E. Horn
The Christian in Modern Style
Pages 2-3[2]

29

Play the Ball As You Find It

As famous Bobby Jones once said to that reporter shortly after his crippling illness was diagnosed for good, twenty years before he died, and knowing he faced debilitation that would one day take his life, "Yes, it's really very bad, and it will not get much better. But I've learned in golf to play the ball as you find it and do the best you can. So let's just play it and talk no more about it." And down the heartbreak of all those many years, he never did. So when tragic illness strikes a man of hearty courage, and he enfolds that suffering to his breast in silence, and takes all the terror, but learns to live whatever's left in spite of it; then and there, in life as well as death, you have a miracle of resurrection.

Richard M. Cromie
Sometime Before the Dawn
Page 27[3]

To Jump Backwards off the Precipice

Picture yourself in a position in which I have been many times as a mountaineer. You are perched high on a rock face, about to begin to rappel. Sixty feet, seventy feet, perhaps hundreds of feet yawn between you and the ground. You have checked the piton to which the rope is attached several times to see if it is secure.

You feel the rope in your hands, and you know from every spec sheet available that the doubled three-eighths-inch nylon strands in your grip have a combined tensile strength of over 8,000 pounds. You don't want to look down, but you glance quickly over your shoulder once more to make sure the rope reaches the ground, or at least another ledge from which to continue to rappel. The rope undulates gently in the breeze beneath you. In a moment it will be tight as piano wire, humming with vibration as you jump out and down on the descent.

Everything is in order. Technically, statistically, your descent is assured. You have told yourself that a hundred times. Now is the moment of truth. Do you believe it — believe it enough to entrust your entire weight to the piton, carabiner, and rope, and to jump back into empty space, suspended like a spider on a thread? The specs on your equipment are mere knowledge now. You've got that in your head. But to *act* on that knowledge, to jump backwards off the precipice — *that* takes more than your head. It takes something lower down — in your stomach, perhaps — called faith.

> *James R. Edwards*
> *"Faith as Noun and Verb"*
> ***Christianity Today***
> *Page 21*[4]

In the Name of God Stop This Madness

In A.D. 391, a Christian named Telemachus became concerned about the depravity of the Roman Empire — the bloodthirsty craving for violence, the gladiators, the Colosseum, the arena. Some of this is not that far removed from the bloodthirsty craving of our society for violent entertainment. Finally, Telemachus could be silent no longer. He jumped out of the stands in the arena in Rome, stood in front of the crowd, lifted his arms in the air, and said, "In the name of God, stop this madness!" The crowd turned on Telemachus and killed him. Telemachus never could have guessed that the Emperor Honorius would be so disturbed by that incident that in a very short time he would sign the imperial edict that ended the brutality of those games.

When I heard the story of Telemachus and thought about the increasing violence and brutality of the society in which we live and of the escalating insanity of the nuclear arms race, something in me asked, "Isn't it time for some Christian somewhere to take the risk of saying, 'In the name of God, stop this madness'?"

Here you see what one person can do.

James A. Harnish
Jesus Makes the Difference
Page 100[5]

We Decided to Go the Other Way

TISHOMINGO, Miss. — David Herbert never expected this. In twenty years of coaching, he's never experienced anything like it. Few high school coaches do.

He has received nothing but praise.

Herbert, 46, coaches in the state's smallest school classification in the remote northeast Mississippi town of Tishomingo.

He fooled everyone including the rulesmakers last Thursday night.

For those who missed it, Tishomingo High led Falkner 16-14 with seven seconds to play. Because of tie-breaking procedures, Tishomingo needed to win by four or more points to advance to the state's playoffs.

With the ball at Falkner's 35, Tishomingo had time for just one play.

And nobody in Tishomingo County can kick a fifty-two-yard field goal.

"We weighed our chances of scoring on one play and knew they weren't good," Herbert said. "We decided to go the other way."

The other way was fifty-five yards backwards for a self-induced safety that tied the score at 16-16 and sent the game into overtime. Tishomingo scored in overtime to win 22-16 for the playoff berth.

"Bizarre Safety Gets Team into State's Playoff"
By Rick Cleveland, Gannett News Service
Marietta Times
November 10, 1988, page 1[6]

Two Kinds of Running

We won't always keep the faith individually or corporately. We will have times when running will be irresistible, as problem after problem piles up on our doorstep. But grace will come to us in such moments, to remind us that there are two kinds of running. One says no, the other, yes.

We have a choice. To run like a deer — afraid of changes we don't understand, afraid of death, afraid of people different from ourselves, afraid of the world — or, to run shepherd-like toward them, toward tomorrow, toward a better day. One will make us a truant; the other a pioneer.

James W. Angell
Accept No Imitations
Pages 126-127[1]

4 — MOTIVATING

Bon Voyage!

Some time ago a friend told me of an occasion when, vacationing in the Bahamas, he saw a large and restless crowd gathered on a pier. Upon investigation he discovered that the object of all the attention was a young man making the last-minute preparations for a solo journey around the world in a homemade boat. Without exception everyone on the pier was vocally pessimistic. All were actively volunteering to tell the ambitious sailor all the things that could possibly go wrong. "The sun will broil you!" "You won't have enough food!" "That boat of yours won't withstand the waves in a storm!" "You'll never make it!"

When my friend heard all these discouraging warnings to the adventurous young man, he felt an irresistible desire to offer some optimism and encouragement. As the little craft began drifting away from the pier toward the horizon, my friend went to the end of the pier, waving both arms wildly like semaphors spelling confidence. He kept shouting: *"Bon Voyage! You're really something! We're with you! We're proud of you! Good luck brother!"*

Sometimes it seems to me that there are two kinds of people. There are those who feel obligated to tell us all the things that can go wrong as we set out over the uncharted waters of our unique lives. Then there are those who stand at the end of the pier, cheering us on, exuding a contagious confidence: *"Bon Voyage!"*

John Powell
Fully Human, Fully Alive
Pages 17-18[1]

35

Home Field Advantage

It is a long and lonely race if you are alone on the field and the bleachers are empty. You might even wonder if it is worth running. It is also disheartening if you succumb to the shadowy thought that your team has deserted you and the bleachers are filled with supporters of the opposition.

People often feel alone, especially after death has visited a household. Sometimes even friends seem distant. Burdens become bigger and obstacles seem more oppressive. At such times we need to reach out and grasp the hand of friends. They will run along side you and share the anxieties of the battle. But there is more! Don't forget the great cloud of witnesses in the bleachers. In the sporting world much talk is made about the advantage of playing on the home field. The friendly crowd can arouse and excite the players on the field to put an extra effort in straining for victory.

The writer of the book of Hebrews gives us the insight of more than present comrades. That innumerable cloud of witnesses which surrounds us reassures us that endurance is possible, that the grace of God will sustain us, and that faith's rewards are eternal. These bleacher saints are not mere spectators of our running, but our witnesses to the faithfulness of our great God. Thus as we run the race on the soil of earth let us remember that we've got the home field advantage. Satan is a squatter; the earth belongs to God. The opposition shouts its doom, but the cheers of the saints drown out their banter.

James R. Bjorge
Living Without Fear
Pages 94-95[2]

Running for My Life

A favorite story told of legendary-and-notably-tough football coach Paul Bryant has to do with one of his players who, in a race down the field in the midst of a big game, overtook an opponent about to score, even though the man with the ball was known to be a faster runner.

Asked to explain his exceptional performance, Bryant's defense player described the fear that turned him into a winner, "That guy was running for a touchdown," he said, "But I was running for my life!"

Among God's many fascinating kinds of gifts is adrenalin. Fear can multiply our strength in emergencies, and there are thousands of case studies to prove it. I'm not sure we are *always* given all the genius or stamina of soul a situation may demand. If that were so, there would be no suicides. But what is beyond question is that, as kites rise before the wind, danger and trouble frequently prompt us to find and utilize emotional reserves that we never knew were there until a crisis called them into play.

James W. Angell
Learning to Manage Our Fears
Page 14[3]

Personal Record

We go, I suppose, because our kids were in age-group track. From the time they were eight or nine through high school graduation, we were accustomed to spending Saturday afternoons sitting lazily in the sun watching the high jump and pole vault pit.

So when the Olympic Track and Field Trials come around each Olympiad, we sign up for the whole nine days of it. We were in Eugene in 1980, Los Angeles in 1984 and Indianapolis in 1988.

Track has a concept that would be helpful in ordinary living: the personal record. One of the women high jump finalists outjumped her personal record twice in the competition. As she cleared each new height, the announcer exclaimed, "This is a new personal record for Mary!" We all cheered like fury, because somehow we were sharing in her thrill of doing the best she had ever done.

It would be nice to have personal bests operating in life. If only an announcer could say, "The sermon we just heard is a personal record for Rev. Perkins," or "That anthem sets a personal record for our choir," or one had a sense after writing a difficult letter, "Hey, that's a personal best for me!" There are many acts in life which deserve commendation."

David Steele
"Personal Record"
The Presbyterian Outlook
August 22-29, 1988
Page 12[4]

Playing the Game
to a Different Audience

At the time one of my best friends was a man named Bud Wilkinson, who was the football coach at the University of Oklahoma in the 1950s, when they won over forty games in a row. It is commonly accepted that he is one of the greatest college coaches of all time.

As I probed around to discover the secret of Bud's success, I learned that he made extensive use of game films. All four quarters would be carefully filmed. This routine of reviewing game films provided a strong reinforcement and motivation, especially since the players knew that their coach — whom they held almost in awe — was seeing in detail everything they might do or try to do.

All of a sudden, I realized why it might be that these players didn't get rattled under pressure. They were playing the game for Bud Wilkinson. They knew that, even if it rained or snowed the day of the game and the crowd in the stands missed the line play, on Sunday Wilkinson was going to see what really happened.

The University of Oklahoma players were playing the game to a different audience! And it suddenly occurred to me that whether or not it was true for that team, it was an important truth for my life. If I could learn to play my life to a different audience — to God, not to people around me — then whether I fouled up or succeeded, I would know God was with me and I wouldn't be alone.

Keith Miller
The Scent of Love
Pages 86-87[5]

The New Generation

While a student at Occidental College during the years immediately following World War II, I was a member of the track team. All international track and field meets had been suspended for the duration of the war, and there were no Olympic Games. However, when the lights went on again all over the world, so did the desire for international competition, in particular, the Olympics.

Our track coach at the time was Payton Jordan, a world record holder in the 100-meter on grass. Still a trim athlete, he was also an internationally recognized coach. He had a way of making champions. Runners came from all over the world to train under him. I can still remember seeing him stride around the infield, his blond hair blowing in the wind, his blue eyes intense with interest and concentration, shouting instructions and encouragement to his athletes. He would take long minutes to explain the finer points of a race, the stride, the strategy, the timing necessary for winning. Encouragement and edification radiated from this coach's heart. No wonder champions loved to train under him. Truly, he was a servant to their emergence even if that meant their shattering his world record. The important thing was the new generation, the strength of the team. God gave us Payton Jordans for the sake of the kingdom.

Louis H. Evans, Jr.
Hebrews, the Communicator's Commentary
Page 221[6]

40

You Are a Significant Person

Always remember that you are a significant person. I am thinking of a man that probably no person who reads this [paragraph] has ever heard of. His name was Karl Downs. He was a Methodist preacher in Oakland, California, who died of a heart attack at an early age. Several years before he died, he was asked by the Juvenile Court to take responsibility for a young man who was always getting into trouble. Karl Downs accepted that responsibility, and in a very kind, loving way he became a substitute father for that boy. I say that you have never heard of Karl Downs, but you have heard of that boy. His name is Jackie Robinson. All of us who like baseball will never forget the tremendous contribution made by the first black man to ever play major league baseball. But had it not been for Karl Downs! He *was* a significant person. I am a significant person; *you* are a significant person; *everybody* is significant."

Charles L. Allen
The Secret of Abundant Living
Page 48[74]

The Impossible Barrier Myth

When our leader exposes us to successful people, it not only inculcates certain values, it also convinces us that if they can achieve, so can we. Seeing another succeed somehow inspires us to succeed. For nine years the record for the mile hovered just above four minutes. As early as 1945, Gunder Haegg had approached the barrier with a time of 4:01.4. But many people said that the limits of physical capacity had been reached and that it was impossible to break that barrier. Then in 1954 Roger Bannister broke the tape at 3:59.4. And what was the result? As soon as the myth of the impossible barrier was dispelled, the four-minute mile was attacked and pierced by many with apparent ease. In almost no time the four-minute achievement was bettered sixty-six times by twenty-six different men! If one dismisses this as merely the power of competition, an important motivational point will be missed. There was just as much competition before the four-minute mile was broken. What the succeeding runners discovered from Bannister was that it could be done. An achievement previously thought impossible was not accessible, and the concrete evidence that success was within reach inspired them on to better and better records.

Alan Loy McGinnis
Bringing Out the Best in People
Pages 97-98[8]

The Role of the Coach

Unfortunately, in some churches the professionals in ministry like to keep their people in the role of spectators. These church pros like to appear all-wise, all-skilled, and all-trained while subjugating the laity to subservient and menial roles in the life of the church. I have often wondered why bankers, engineers, and other professionals are given no more responsibility in some churches than ushering. I wonder why educators in daily life become spectators of religious education in church life where their expertise is seldom requested or appreciated.

I also wonder why many church leaders do not encourage their people to read, study, think, and grow. Perhaps it is because they do not want their own position challenged by the supposed casual observers of the faith. I believe that pastors should insist that their people read and study what they are reading and studying. I seldom see a pastor holding a book up on a Sunday morning and saying, "I want all of you to purchase this book today at our book table in the lobby and begin reading it this week. Talk about it to one another. It is exciting and challenging, and it will help you to grow." Is there a fear among professionals that parishioners will be as well-informed about matters of the faith as they are? Some blame for lethargy among the players could be due to lack of challenge from the coaches.

Jim Smoke
Whatever Happened to Ordinary Christians?
Pages 56-57[9]

43

Climbing a Majestic Mountain

When the 23rd Olympic Games came to the United States, the doomsayers predicted a disaster. In everyone's minds were the terrorist attacks which made Munich a tragedy and the fiscal disaster in Montreal, which left the government one billion dollars in debt.

But the U.S. games proved to be a smashing success, in large part due to Peter Ueberroth, the forty-two-year-old optimist who masterminded the triumph and turned in a surplus of more than $200 million.

Ueberroth made speech after speech to the 72,000 Olympic workers (about half of them volunteers) about how together they had to climb a majestic mountain. Such language might sound corny to some, but there was no question in anyone's mind that Ueberroth saw it exactly that way. Such commitment to the cause could also make him imperious with those whose dedication did not seem adequate. One day in the headquarters cafeteria he stopped to talk to some employees who were having lunch. The chat was pleasantly routine until one of the women asked about possible salary increases. Ueberroth, the unsalaried volunteer, turned cold and snapped: "You shouldn't be working here if you don't understand what we are trying to do."

Alan Loy McGinnis
Bringing Out the Best in People
Pages 65-66[10]

5 — PLAYING

You've Got to Enjoy This Kind of Thing

Gary Demarest, a Presbyterian pastor in California and an old friend, tells about watching a USC football game. USC is, incidentally, his alma mater. In the last few seconds, near the goal line and with one play left, USC called a timeout. The press picked up the fact that when the quarterback ran over to see the coach, they both began to laugh up-roariously. The quarterback came back, and they ran the play. The press wanted to know what had so amused the two men. It seems the coach had called the quarterback over simply to say, "If you play football, you've got to enjoy this kind of thing!"

If you want to enjoy the Christian life (the most exciting game there is and one played for the highest stakes of all), you've got to learn to enjoy the hard things along with the good things. Rejoice.

Bruce Larson
A Call to Holy Living
Page 85[1]

Playing With God

For Jesus' followers today, fostering a spirit of playfulness is a momentous challenge. Even salvaging genuine play for children taxes the ingenuity of parents and teachers. Walking through a toy section in a store can be revealing and frustrating. So many toys emphasize the violence of our culture. The countless hours spent by children and by adults watching television are another obstacle to playfulness. Passive spectators rarely become creative players.

Yet God continues to be a playful God, longing to play with the other children of God. Only in a genuine prayer life can we discover, and enjoy, the playfulness of God. Only in a genuine prayer life can God nurture a spirit of playfulness in us.

In the busyness of our lives we long for recreation, for re-creative play. Even more does our Creator God long to play with us. Playing with God, and with one another, is the key to genuine Sabbath rest. Can there be holiness without this holy rhythm in life, this sacred time for play?

Shakespeare was right! "The play's the thing." Play is the thing we need if we are to be called children of God. There seems to be no other way to enter the kingdom.

Carol Frances Jergen
"The Play's the Thing"
Lutheran Woman Today
Volume 2, March 1989
Pages 7-8[2]

Kill-Joy Talk

Recreation is an important ingredient for happy living. Those who have learned the thrill of skiing in fresh-powder snow are in danger of becoming ski bums and sacrifice other joys just to spend a few hours on the slopes. Very few of us are financially able to spend all the time we'd like enjoying our favorite sport.

We have to learn to put priorities on our time, our money, our physical stamina, and even the patience of our families. What do we really want? Can we afford that new boat, the trailer, and the water-skiing equipment without jeopardizing our budget in other departments,or perhaps our children's future education?

On the surface, any talk about temperance appears to be a wet blanket. It sounds like kill-joy talk, like prohibitions, and no-nos which are meant to lessen one's joy of life. And this is a tough psychological obstacle to get around. In a sense, *it is kill-joy talk.* We are talking about killing lesser joys to obtain greater joys, like the athlete who kills his enjoyment of sweets to enjoy a place on the varisty team. It merely becomes a matter of deciding what we really want and acting accordingly.''

Orien Johnson
Becoming Transformed
Pages 74-75[3]

All Joy to Work

The wrench of loving baseball is that we live with and for those lovely lads for more than six months of the year. They become close friends. Work schedules are made to conform to their activities, and then it is over. Sportswriters who glowed and suffered with them all summer suddenly find their very names obnoxious. Silence falls. The long winter sets in. They are the same as dead.

But now the men are exercising, spring training has begun, and so has life again.

I am working now night and day to fit together the assorted research materials I have collected so that I can begin to plot my novel. I really am terribly busy these days, but the incentive is at hand. It is all joy to work hard now, during spring training, because soon, oh, soon an umpire will bellow: "Play ball" and the fun will begin. Work will not seem like work.

Eugenia Price
At Home on St. Simons
Page 62[4]

The Main Thing . . . Fun

It is ironic to think that I should come to this college to be the chaplain, to represent the Christian faith, and when I leave, I am memorialized as the lacrosse coach.

It is interesting to reflect that in some ways the most personally satisfying and perhaps even the most effective ministry that I have carried on here has been outside the church and totally beyond any formal ecclesiastical relationship. I am just a guy with other guys who happens to know more about lacrosse than they do. Therefore, for two hours every day for two months we get together. The most important thing in our lives at those moments is a little ball, the cradling of it and tossing it around. We don't have a great team, but it has been getting better each year, and this year we had four wins to three losses. The main thing, though, has been the fun we have all had in it.

Anyway, this lacrosse trophy has come to symbolize, for me, all the fun that there is in natural human associations — having a good time together, gathering around a common enterprise, just simply tossing a ball back and forth with some of the nicest guys. I reflect upon the goodness of life in these associations.

John P. Coburn
Twentieth-Century Spiritual Letters
Pages 65-66[5]

Mini-vacations from Routine Existence

Ten or twelve people in my church's youth group had come to the hall on this Sunday night because I had been tricked. A denominational authority figure whom I respect had advised me that youth groups are more likely to flourish if they help plan their own programs. Consequently, I had asked for suggestions at a regualr Sunday night meeting. "Basketball," those with the loudest voices had responded. I had tried to think of legitimate reasons why this was a poor idea, but I could not come up with enough objections quickly enough.

And so there we were.

I sat watching group members play. If ministry is aimed at producing a future generation of church leaders, then I am probably not really conducting a young ministry at all, I thought. If the evening of basketball was supposed to be a form of recruitment for creeds and church boards, then it was undoubtedly wasted.

However, if ministry is service to and affirmation of individuals; if ministry is sowing seeds that may grow without — or in spite of — our constant efforts; if ministry is providing a place in which people may take mini-vacations from routine existence, then perhaps this small, chaotic group in a chilly, drab room, engaged in a game that has become increasingly disorganized, is a thoroughly legitimate form of ministry.

Andrew Gilman
"The Name of the Game"
Christian Ministry
July 1987
Pages 21, 23[6]

The Stadium as Cathedral

To the twentieth-century mind, the idea of play and games as worship rituals is almost incredible. Play has been secularized too long. What we find so incredible is that something so frivolous and pleasurable as play could integrally be tied to the serious matter of worship.

True worship is unproductive, nonutilitarian. A worshipful attitude is an attitude caught up in adoration and praise and celebration. It seeks nothing. It is, by human standards, a wasteful procedure.

Worship also is something we engage in voluntarily, a matter of free choice and free will. One cannot be forced to worship in a meaningful way any more than one can be forced to play.

Worship also exists in our leisure time, the time not allocated for work.

These structural similarities between worship and play may point us in a good direction for reforming sport. The integration of sport and genuine Christianity is possible only when we recognize the potential for sport as a celebrative and worshipful act. (And not simply as a platform for evangelism or the building of character.) Play can be an expression of inner calm, a peace-in-action, known only to those who have understandable cause (the grace of God) for celebration.

Shirl J. Hoffman
"The Sanctification of Sport"
Christianity Today
April 4, 1986
Page 19[7]

Taking Ourselves Lightly

The real object of play is to discover newness in our lives. In play, we open ourselves to a powerful creative energy. When we dare to dabble, unique things can happen. The unexpected. The unpredictable. Play propels us into work with renewed strength and ingenuity.

Can serious people learn to play? I certainly hope so. It would be sad to think that only a few silly people are allowed access to this rarely discussed gift of the Spirit. I have heard it said that the angels can fly because they take themselves lightly. This is the essence of play. Through play comes the freedom to allow the stiff wind of the Holy Spirit to blow through our too-often stuffy and serious lives, tugging at our clothes and messing up our hair.

The God who created a perfectly synchronized universe also took time to fashion and paint each bird, to design each cloud formation, and to give us the gift of laughter. These are not the actions of an all-work-and-no-play God. The God of detail and delight, the God of mountain and mud puddle can expect nothing less of us, for we are creations of God's own hand.

Lori Johnson Rosenkvist
"Playing Works"
Lutheran Women Today
Volume 2, Number 3, 1989
Page 10[8]

6 — PERSEVERING

Get Up and Finish the Race

[Jim] Ryun was a favorite in the Olympic 1,500 meters the day he fell. As a massive crowd in the stadium and on television watched, Ryun made his way around the track in a pack of finely conditioned runners. And then he crashed to the ground. In a race of that sort, a fall virtually guarantees that it will be impossible to win. And Jim Ryun must have known that as he lay there on the track.

What were the options Ryun sorted through his mind in that moment? Quitting and heading for the locker room and a hot shower? Anger at having trained for so long for this event and now missing the chance for the gold medal? Self-pity over the seeming bad deal he'd gotten by being jostled in the pack?

None of these, apparently. Rather he seems to have had only one thought that eclipsed all these possibilities I've mentioned. Getting up and running again; *finishing,* even if he couldn't win. *And that is what Jim Ryun did.* He got up and ran again. Others won medals, but Ryun won a large measure of respect when he determined to finish the race.

> Gordon MacDonald
> ***Rebuilding Your Broken World***
> *Page 221*[1]

Not as Expected

In the movie *The Natural,* Robert Redford plays a promising young baseball player at the turn of the century who leaves his small midwestern town to head for the big leagues. On his journey to the big time he is shot by a psychotic athlete killer and drops out of life for sixteen years. He then makes another go at baseball, even though it could kill him due to his earlier wound. He eventually, having become famous, meets up with Glenn Close, his home town fiancee whom he'd never sent for. After some nervous small talk, she looks across the table at him with painful concern and asks, "What happened to you, Roy?" Redford fidgets, looks out the window, and finally says after an uncomfortable silence, "life just didn't turn out like I expected."

We ask, "Was I wrong to expect so much from you, God? Was I wrong to expect so much for my life?"

And there comes an answer: "I do have good news for you. But it is in the form of a cross and an empty tomb. It is an unusual vision, I must admit, and one in which many who are faint-hearted will stumble and fall. But the righteous one will live by its reliability."

Andre Resner, Jr.
"A Year of Lament"
The Princeton Seminary Bulletin
Volume IX, Number 2, 1989
Page 162[2]

Pressing On

I asked an Olympic runner the secret of his success. His answer had profound implications for the Christian life.

This is what the runner said: "The only way to win a race is to forget all previous victories, which would give you false pride and all former failures which would give you false fears. Each race is a new beginning. Pressing on to the finish tape is all that's important!"

This young man knew what he was talking about. He was right about athletic running and spiritual living.

The freedom to forget is a gift of the Master. He frees us to forget past achievements and failures so that we can press ahead to the goal.

Lloyd John Ogilvie
Let God Love You
Page 110[3]

The Iron Horse

They called him the iron horse. Year after year, injured or well, Lou Gehrig never missed a game for the New York Yankees. He played with lumbago, a concussion, even broken bones.

Then, at the start of the 1939 season, Lou suddenly became slow and awkward in the field, ineffectual at bat. In a game with the Washington Senators, he went to bat four times and never even nicked the ball. He also muffed an easy throw. That's when he told manager, Joe McCarthy, "I guess the time has come to take me out." His consecutive game record ended at 2,130, a record that may never be equaled.

Doctors discovered that Lou had a rare and fatal disease called *amyotrophic lateral sclerosis.* The next two years, as life ebbed from him, he refused to give in to the disease.

On July 4, 1939, Lou was honored at Yankee Stadium. The spectators fell silent as Gehrig stepped to the microphone and said, "I may have been given a bad break, but I've got an awful lot to live for: I consider myself the luckiest man on the face of the earth." It was the most heartwarming and inspiring moment in the history of baseball.

Dale E. Galloway
Expect a Miracle
Pages 60-61[4]

Full Circle

When our three children Anne, Jon and Elizabeth were very young, I taught them to ski. In the beginning everything they knew depended on my wise and authoritative instruction. Now we have come full circle; each of them is a better skier than I and they now teach me. They watch my form and make helpful suggestions. I would be a fool not to benefit from this good and necessary change of place within the obedience cycle.

There are, however, parents who have just this problem of adult isolation and stubbornness as their sons and daughters move into adolescence. That's because they as parents are trying to live with fourteen-year-olds as if they were seven. Living with the cycle takes skill, but the rewards are wonderful — and not only in skiing.

Earl Palmer
The 24-Hour Christian
Pages 125-126[5]

Game Plan

In game play it has always been my philosophy to follow our game plan. If we do believe in it, we will wear the opposition down and will get to them. If we break away from our style, however, and play their style, we're in trouble. And if we let our emotions command the game rather than our reason, we will not function effectively.

I constantly caution our teams: "Play your game, just play your game. Eventually, if you play, stick to your style, class will tell in the end." This does not mean that we will always outscore our opponent, but does insure that we will not beat ourselves.

John Wooden, as told to Jack Tobin
They Call Me Coach
Page 111[6]

More Beautiful Every Year

The athlete who lives for the fun of games faces the inevitable law of diminishing returns. The athletic life is short. The baseball player has to retire while still in his prime. He is soon incapacitated to compete with younger men. I do not know any exception to this rule in the world or in the realm of matter. But in the spiritual world it is exactly the opposite. The satisfactions may be small at the start, but they grow greater. It is as the song says, "sweeter as the years go by." Those saintly old men and women, with their radiant smiles, are reflecting a life experience which grew more beautiful every year. There is nothing to compare to the blessing and peace of one who has walked with Christ for a lifetime.

Frank C. Laubach
Channels of Spiritual Power
Page 136[7]

7 — PROJECTING

The Right Direction

It must have been from my father that I learned the love of games that has stayed with me all my life. I remember the golf we played in Hamilton every week. He had, in his youth, been a notable shinty player. (With apologies to the highlanders, I should explain that shinty is a kind of primitive hockey.) He played golf as if it were shinty. I don't suppose he ever hit a ball more than a hundred fifty yards. But I doubt if he was ever off the fairway in all his playing days.

So, when I was majestically dispatching the ball large distances to all the points of the compass except the right one, he would give it three sharp raps up the fairway on the green and sink the putt. As we left the tee, he for the middle of the fairway, I for the wilds, he would say smugly: "See you at the green!" and go on his undeviating way. I thereby learned the useful lesson that, however far you go, it is not much use if it is not in the right direction.

William Barclay
A Spiritual Autobiography
Pages 3-4[1]

Losing Sight of the Finish

Hamsters in cages run the rat race. They get in their wheels and run nine thousand miles, but never get anywhere. And it can be like that in the church: endless committee meetings and activities, routines and procedures that we do over and over. They may have the value, but have become for us a rat race to the point that we forget the goal.

A haunting analogy of this misdirected running can be drawn from the 1984 Olympics. A female marathon runner came into the arena with all her energy and strength depleted. As she staggered into the arena it was obvious that she was on automatic pilot. The legs were pumping simply because in the past they had been taught to pump. But her eyes were glazed over and she didn't know where the finish line was. Sometimes it is the same in the church. We forget our resources, we lose sight of the finish line, the goal toward which we run.

Roberta Louis Hestenes
"Renewal Amidst the Darkness"
The Power to Make Things New
Edited by Bruce Larson
Page 88[2]

Maturity

Time always reminds us of aging, and aging always depresses us. Two famous baseball players have given us good advice on the subject. Toward the end of his career pitcher Lefty Grove said, "I'm throwing it just as hard as I ever did, but it doesn't get there as fast as it used to." That's a common experience of life. But Casey Stengel has even better advice for us. He said, "The trick is growing up without growing old." Some people never seem to grow up. Others never seem to grow old. Maturity is another name for growing up without growing old. It's a worthy goal.

Robert C. Shannon
"Let Me Illustrate"
Pulpit Digest
January-February, 1988
Page 65[3]

Living Out a Dream

The story of a life-style change that grabs me most is the story of Robert Manry, recorded in his book, *Tinkerbelle*. The story is close to me, because Manry lived in Cleveland, Ohio. I was raised in Cleveland, and as a boy I delivered The (Cleveland) *Plain Dealer*. Robert Manry worked for the *Plain Dealer* as a copy-editor. At forty-seven, Manry decided he had to do some things with his life that were fun. He never dreamed, though, that they would lead to a change in his total life-style.

On June 1, 1965, Manry, in his little white boat with the red sail, left Falmouth, Massachusetts, bound for Falmouth, England, some three thousand miles away. He spent the next seventy-eight days on the high seas with all of the joys and terrors of sailing. He was swept overboard; he experienced fear, hallucinations, and loneliness. He almost turned back, but finally arrived at his destination and was greeted by nearly 50,000 people. Those people were not there to see history being made; they were there because they identified with Manry's dream. "The voyage was something I simply had to do," Manry told the world.

The notoriety and new sources of income cut Manry free from the bondage he had experienced as a mundane copy-editor. For the rest of his life, he lived this new life-style that came about as he was willing to live out one of his dreams.

Jim Conway
Men in Midlife Crisis
Pages 90-91[4]

Bleacher Bums

Have you ever sat so far away from the action on a baseball field that you would have had a better view in front of your television set at home? You squint in the sunlight from the far reaches of the left field stands and notice that there are a host of people sitting right behind homeplate — the best seats in the stadium. You confess to a great deal of envy and wish that you were important enough to own season tickets to those select quarters. Often it is the rich, famous, and very important people in our world who occupy those seats. Many of us bleacher bums would give a lot to sit where those people sit. They have the best of the best and we look upon them with envy.

The ordinary Christian and the ordinary baseball fan have a lot in common. Both seem to want conditions to be far better than they are. There is apparently little contentment in knowing that others have a better seat in the kingdom of God than you do.

Ordinary Christians should highly esteem those whom God places in leadership positions within the Christian community. But we should not tolerate those leaders who install themselves as pedestal people or Christian gurus. Our identity is not linked to our position or associations. Our identity is founded in who we are in Christ Jesus.

Ordinary Christians aren't looking for the best seat. But they are looking for God's place for them!

Jim Smoke
Whatever Happened to Ordinary Christians?
Pages 163, 167, 169[5]

Running a Race We've Already Won

The goal for Paul's race was Christ. Christ was the finish tape for him. A winning runner forgets the opponents around or behind him and looks only at the goal. Paul was in prison when he wrote to forget the past and focused on the next steps toward the goal. He had an indomitable trust in the Lordship of Christ over past and future time. He longed to become more like Christ in every thought and action.

The race of the Christian life is the only race that is run knowing we have won already.

Lloyd John Ogilvie
Let God Love You
Page 112[6]

If You Build It, He Will Come

When Mark, the cynical brother-in-law in the movie *Field of Dreams*, tells Ray Kinsella that he mustn't sell the farm, we witness a quiet shift in this delightful story of baseball, belief and wonder. Until this moment, Mark has assumed that his sister's family is slightly bonkers. They are, after all, insisting that the baseball field Ray has constructed on his Iowa farm is being used by Shoeless Joe Jackson and other players from the notorious 1919 Chicago White Sox, the team on which eight members were charged with deliberately losing the World Series.

Kinsella (played by Kevin Costner) and his wife, Annie (Amy Madigan), are products of the 1960s; they decide to keep their '60s dream alive by growing corn on an idyllic Iowa farm. Life on the farm is interrupted when Ray hears a voice quietly telling him, "If you build it, he will come." The beauty of the story emerges from the cautious manner in which Ray, joined by his trusting family, decides to plow up valuable corn acreage in what to doubting neighbors looks about as sensible as Noah's decision to build an ark. But like Noah, Ray has no choice. He feels compelled to follow the voice, the source of which he takes on faith.

The central wisdom of the film (and the novel) is that if one can break out of the confines of modern rationality, it is possible to experience a power that is not limited to the time-space continuum we call reality.

James M. Wall
"A Playing Field for the Boys of Eternity"
The Christian Century
May 17, 1989
Page 515[7]

8 — LOSING

Emphasize With His Humiliations

What can we do to instill a sense of worth in our children that will minimize the seductiveness of tooth-and-claw competition? We can try to enable them to have some experiences that are closely analogous as possible to experience of the grace of God.

Jimmy may be a champion speller, but when it comes to gym, he consistently places last. Being often humiliated, he "hates" gym. His tendency is to find his sense of worth in connection with the more intellectual activities and simply avoid the athletic whenever he can. If you are a person who places a very high value on athletic prowess, you may have a hard time not feeling disappointed in your boy. In fact, you may even nag him and try to push him — even shame him — into greater accomplishments. If you do these things you are training him for the spirituality of tooth and claw.

No doubt, he will not make his claws out of athletics, but he will look for some way in which to establish himself, since he will not feel established in grace. It seems to me that the correct strategy is to give Jimmy the sense that you empathize with his humiliations, that you, at any rate, are with him in his failures. Thus you reflect, in a dim and distant way, the everlasting arms of the Father of mercies, who comforts us in all our affliction.

Robert C. Roberts
"The Sanctification of Sport:
Competition and Compassion"
Christianity Today
April 4, 1986
Page 23[1]

So Many Pieces to Play With

Life does resemble a huge game, and all the things we have, know, and do are like so many pawns which we manipulate in an effort to win. There are never enough pawns. Each individual chooses his pawns, or rather uses those he has available — his body or his mind, his health or sickness, his family, titles, reputation, wealth. In this way the ego is enlarged to include all its pawns in order to increase its chances.

It is not enough, of course, to have pawns. One must also know how to use them. And the more one has, the more difficult this is — and the more ignominious it would be to fail with so many pieces to play with! So it is that many people deny their talents, both to escape the responsibility that goes with them, and to insure against possible failure. The reason why so many people take pleasure in thinking and talking about their past misfortunes and the injustices they have suffered is partly to excuse themselves for not winning at every move as they would have liked, to make it clear that they have been laboring under a handicap. At times this attitude can verge on hypochondria.

Paul Tournier
The Adventure of Living
Pages 99-100[2]

The Wallenda Factor

Karl Wallenda lived on top of the world. The aerialist thrilled crowds with his daring stunts on the high wire before that fateful day in 1978 when his show ended. Wallenda plunged 75 feet to his death before an audience of thousands in San Juan, Puerto Rico.

What happened? His widow explained that Karl had never been one to know fear. Self-confidence marked his style until he started worrying. Little details of safety preoccupied his mind. He checked and double-checked the tightrope to make certain that everything was secure.

This was a different Karl. For the first time, instead of putting his energies into walking the wire, he concentrated on *not falling*. From then on Wallenda became an accident just waiting to happen. It was inevitable that he fall, or so his widow now feels.

Motivational speakers and managers now call this the Wallenda factor. Beware of being so afraid of failure that you dwell on the negatives. If so, you will succeed only in the ultimate negative, which is nothing.

Life is a risk we must take. Be careful in a prudent sort of way, but don't be paralyzed by a fear of failure. In Jesus Christ we can be positive and progress on!

C. W. Bess
"Homiletic Bias"
Pulpit Digest
March-April 1988
Page 66[3]

Penthouse or Outhouse

In typical fashion, when George Allen moved to Washington, D.C., as head coach of the Redskins, he promised the nation's capital the moon.

The team had a brilliant pre-season that first year. Then, early in the regular season, they won several amazing victories. It appeared the Redskins were to be lifted from their common role of loser to the uncommon role of winner. As time passed, however, the inevitable occurred. They began to lose and lose and lose. The blame fell, at least in part, not on Coach George Allen, but on a quarterback named Sonny Jurgenson. Jurgenson possesses a quality I deeply admire: personal security. It seems as though no one can intimidate Sonny Jurgenson.

One day after another defeat, Sonny was getting ready to take a shower and go home. A sportswriter leaned over to him in the locker room and said, "Say, Sonny, be honest now. Don't all these off-the-wall remarks we write and all this public flack disturb you? Doesn't it make you want to quit when people throw things at you from the stands and when you get those dirty letters?"

Sonny leaned back, gave a big, toothless grin, and sighed, "No, not really. I don't want to quit. I've been in this game long enough to know that every quarterback, every week of the season, spends his time either in the penthouse or in the outhouse."

Charles R. Swindoll
Hand Me Another Brick
Page 93[4]

His Lust to Be Number One

There's an ancient Greek legend that illustrates beautifully the plight of combative competition. In one of the important races, a certain athlete ran well, but he still placed second. The crowd applauded the winner noisly, and after a time a statue was erected in his honor. But the one who had placed second came to think of himself as a loser. Corrosive envy ate away at him physically and emotionally, filling his body with stress. He could think of nothing else but his defeat and his lust to be number one, and he decided he had to destroy the statue that was a daily reminder of his lost glory.

A plan took shape in his mind, which he began cautiously to implement. Late each night, when everyone was sleeping, he went to the statue and chiseled at the base hoping to so weaken the foundation that eventually it would topple. One night, as he was chiseling the sculpture in violent and envious anger, he went too far. The heavy marble statue teetered on its fragile base and crashed down on the disgruntled athlete. He died beneath the crushing weight of the marble replica of the one he had grown to hate. But in reality he had been dying long before, inch by inch, chisel blow by chisel blow. He was the victim of his own stressful, competitive envy.

Lloyd J. Ogilvie
Making Stress Work For You
Pages 101-102 [5]

You Always Have a Choice

Eight-year-old Tommie was bragging to his dad about what a great hitter he was becoming. His dad took him out in the backyard to give him an opportunity to demonstrate his new-found hitting ability. When they got in the backyard, Tommie's dad said, "Go ahead and show me what you can do." With a confident grin, Tommie threw the ball in the air, swung at it, and missed. "Strike one," said his dad. Knowing he could hit the ball, Tommie threw it in the air again, and missed. "Strike two," laughed his father. And again, "Strike three."

Not to be beaten, Tommie said, "Boy, am I a great pitcher."

No matter what happens to you, you still have a choice. There is no such thing as a choiceless life. You *always* have a choice! For example, suppose someone does something that hurt you. What has happened is external, outside of you. Your reaction that takes place on the inside is your own. You respond, "But I can't do anything about what has happened to me." Right there you have given up without a fight. You can do something. Your reaction to what has happened is still your own choice. How you choose to react is the one thing that no one can take away from you.

Dale E. Galloway
Expect a Miracle
Page 109[6]

9 — WINNING

Victories Are Crucial

No matter who we are, or where we live, victories are crucial — victories in all sizes.

Victories are important for political candidates, baseball pitchers, and nations. They have to do with the diagnosis of cancer and with high school or college graduation.

We stand up and shout, "We're number one!" Or we declare a public holiday, make a "V" with our second and third fingers, or give trophies to one another. Or tell stories to our grandchildren — Moses escapes from Pharaoh at the Red Sea; David slays the nine-foot Philistine giant, Goliath . . . Bob, a high school student, failed a couple of courses and began to be down on himself. Then he made the football team and, in his senior year, made the all-star team. The heart came back into him when that happened. Young people need victories to help them believe in themselves. All of us need victories.

James W. Angell
Accept No Imitations
Pages 128-129[1]

Just Another Victory Ceremony?

Shelley Mann, the American girl, stood to receive her gold medal at the Olympic Stadium. There was an American girl on her right and an American girl on her left. Tears were running down her cheeks as she stood there tall, straight and beautiful. Just another victory ceremony? Not really.

There was a time when Shelley Mann could scarcely move a muscle, much less stand. Stricken with polio at age five, Shelley began going to a swimming pool, not to become a champion swimmer, but just to get a little strength back into her feeble arms and legs. At first she was held up by the buoyancy of the water. She cried tears of joy the day she was able to lift an arm out of the water — a major triumph. Her first goal was to swim the width of the pool, then the pool's length. As she reached each goal, she set new ones. She swam two lengths, three lengths, and then four lengths.

Shelley Mann went on to become one of the greats among American female swimmers. She was the world record holder in all 100- and 200-meter butterfly events and won the 100-meter butterfly at the 1956 Melbourne Olympics.

The girl who at one time couldn't even hold her head up, the girl who had to fight just to lift an arm out of the water, was the same girl who won the Gold Medal in the most difficult butterfly stroke. Just another victory? Not really.

Howard E. Ferguson
The Edge
Pages 2-9[2]

74

God's Desire is To Win People

[The] problem with prayer is increasingly accentuated for me the longer I am associated as a chaplain with university athletics. After a recent game, for example, numerous people were saying things like, "You should have prayed harder, Father" or "Well, your prayers didn't work today, did they?"

When my prayers do work, as, say, in a thrilling come-from-behind victory, what am I supposed to think? That the prayers of the opposing fans didn't work? The God I believe in doesn't cause fumbles or help with freethrows, and His Mother isn't specially assigned to assist fourth-quarter heroics of Catholic quarterbacks. God doesn't win games. Men and women do. God's desire is to win people.

William Toohey
Life After Birth: Spirituality For College Students
Pages 60-61[3]

Not Forgetting the Message

Some years ago a cartoon appeared in the *Saturday Review* that was a parody on the ancient Greek runner who brought the news from Marathon that his people had been victorious. Twenty-six miles he had raced alone with that newsworthy headline that the Greeks had conquered a superior army of Persians. And, as you recall the history of that event, you will remember that it took every last ounce of energy, for he arrived at the waiting crowd with just enough left to whisper, "Victory," and he fell exhausted in a dead heap on the ground. But the cartoon had a different version. It pictured the same group of Athenians waiting anxiously for the news; but at the end they were rewarded by a rather silly looking little runner, with spindly legs and sagging body, who raced all the way up to them and stumbled to the finish, only to say, "Uh, uh, I forgot the message." Twenty-six miles of steady running to get to the great moment and he forgot what he was supposed to say. Pity the poor creature, who gave his all, only to forget the good news that all was well at Marathon.

And, what do we say, now that we are here? Are you prepared with the original runner to shout out the single word of "Victory"; or will you, as the cartoon substitute, whimper out a confused, "Uh, uh, I forgot the message."

Richard M. Cromie
Sometime Before the Dawn
Pages 68-69[4]

to do

July 5 — Dick Doyle — Sat AM

5 — Call Dave F ✓
    Dave P ✓

3

INFo — Lodge 7¼
    July 12 — 8 P

Homemade
ice cream

4 — ⟨Library Books — BACK⟩

5 — Mary Ellen — ✓

6 — Telephone Bill ?

7 — Summer — to do ⟩ SAT

8 — ⟨Ad   7   card out
   Finance 6 —⟩

⟨ Noth 15 Th No Financ
  Noth 8 = No Worship

For your
information

Mon ~~Sept~~ 12
~~July 12~~ - 8 PM

VAN Buren FTAM #711 -

on MAIN Street -

- ~~Easter~~ ~~Mason~~ Regular Meeting

- Refreshment will be Served
  ~~Homemade Ice Cream~~ after
  Meeting

MartuMasni are invited.

Class

Class never runs scared. It is sure-footed and confident in the knowledge that you can meet life head-on and handle whatever comes along.

Jacob had it. Esau didn't. Symbolically, we can look to Jacob's wrestling match with the angel. Those who have class have wrestled with their own personal angel and won a victory that marks them thereafter.

Class never makes excuses. It takes its lumps and learns from past mistakes.

Class is considerate of others. It knows that good manners are nothing more than a series of petty sacrifices.

Class bespeaks an aristocracy that has nothing to do with ancestors or money. The most affluent blueblood can be totally without class while the descendant of a Welsh miner may ooze class from every pore.

Class never tries to build itself up tearing others down.

Class is already up and need not strive to look better by making others look worse.

If you have class, you don't need much of anything else. If you don't have it, no matter what else you have — it doesn't make much difference.

Howard E. Ferguson
The Edge
Page 1-1[5]

The Heavyweight Championship of the Universe

Calvary is judo. The enemy's own power is used to defeat him. Satan's craftily orchestrated plot, rolled along according to play by his agents Judas, Pilate, Herod, and Caiaphas, culminating in the death of God. And this very event, Satan's conclusion, was God's premise. Satan's end was God's means. It saved the world. Christians celebrate the greatest evil and the greatest tragedy of all time as Good Friday. In the symbolic language of Revelation, the meek little lamb *(arnion)* defeats the great and terrible Beast *(therion)* in the last battle, the fight for the heavyweight championship of the universe, by shedding his own blood. Satan's bloody plan became the means of his own despoilment. God won Satan's captives — us — back to himself by freely dying in our place.

It is, of course, the most familiar, the most often-told story in the world. Yet it is also the strangest, and it has never lost its strangeness, its awe, and will not even in eternity, where angels tremble to gaze at things we yawn at. And however strange, it is the only key that fits the lock of our tortured lives and needs.

Peter Kreeft
Making Sense of Suffering
Pages 132-133[6]

My Greatest Achievement

At the beginning of my junior year in high school I had the world in the palm of my hand, I thought. I was playing first string both ways on the football team, I was vice-president of the class, and I was dating a senior cheerleader. Wow, I had it made! During the seventh game of our football season I was clipped. This ended my football and wrestling careers and ultimately resulted in my having to have knee surgery. I went into the hospital one day, was to have surgery the next day and be out as good as new in a week. Well, it just didn't work out that way. I was out in a week, but was back in the next week with complications. My incisions had burst and I had developed a bad staph infection. My dreams and aspirations were going down the drain very quickly. I really wasn't sure where to turn. It was at this point that I let someone besides Tim Cloyd take over. I just could not hold on any longer. Christ lifted me up, and I felt his presence and his love everyday. He worked through my Christian friends and family. After six weeks of hospitalization and a second surgery to clean up the infection, I was released. I had missed ten weeks of school, but I had learned more during that time than I ever could have in school. Christ had taught me through this that sports and achievements are important, but any accomplishment is important only if it glorifies God.

Tim Cloyd
quoted in Betty Shannon Cloyd
Glory Beyond All Comparison
Page 57[1]

Pandemonium Broke Loose

All of our black neighbors came to see daddy when the second Joe Louis-Max Schmeling fight was to take place. There was intense interest, and they asked if they could listen to the fight. We propped the radio in the open window of our house, and we and our visitors sat and stood under a large mulberry tree nearby.

There were heavy racial overtones encompassing the fight, with Joe Louis given a good chance to become the new black heavyweight champion of the world. He had lost in his first boxing encounter with Schmeling, but in this return match Louis almost killed his opponent in the first round.

My father was deeply disappointed in the outcome.

There was no sound from anyone in the yard, except a polite, "Thank you, Mister Earl," offered to my father.

Then, our several dozen visitors filed across the dirt road, across the railroad track, and quietly entered a house about a hundred yards away out in the field. At that point, pandemonium broke loose inside the house, as our black neighbors shouted and yelled in celebration of the Louis victory. But all the curious, accepted proprieties of a racially-segregated society had been carefully observed.

Jimmy Carter
Why Not the Best?
Pages 36-37[8]

Let Me Be What I Can Be

Later today I'll be bringing the invocation at the opening ceremonies for the Fargo Regional Special Olympics. I want to feel the atmosphere of the area, so this morning's run finds me circling the New Field House at North Dakota State University where the festivities will take place.

One hundred and sixty young women and men will recite the Special Olympic Oath after I say my words. Mayor Lindgren will lead us. It goes like this:

"Let me be what I can be.

Let me do what I can do."

I'm grateful to the Kennedy family for developing the Special Olympics. I don't know how anyone can participate in these events and not feel deeply moved. I like the idea of having official huggers, volunteers who hug each person when they have finished their race or swim. That way everyone wins.

Roger Prescott
The Second Mile
Page 78[9]

10 — WITNESSING

The Sound of Bagpipes

The finish of any marathon can be (an) emotional experience.

For a friend of mine the setting was the Scottish Games at Grandfather Mountain. The marathon there is one of the most difficult in this country. It's 26.2 miles through mountainous country test a runner as almost no other race does.

My friend survived that test and ultimately conquered the course. And when he came to the last climb where the finish was supposed to be, he heard the sound of bagpipes. Now, as everyone knows, the skirling of bagpipes stirs passions and emotions inaccessible in other ways. So my friend, already overcome by reaching the end of this ordeal, was in tears when he breasted the hill.

And now he saw he was on a great plain encircled by the camps of the various Scottish clans. And each sent up a great shout as he passed them.

What place he took, he sometimes forgets. But he will never forget when time stood still on that plain atop Grandfather Mountain and all around him were happy cheering people and the sound of bagpipes.

All this has, of course, nothing to do with winning and losing. Winning and losing is what you do in team games. The runner is not in a game; he is in a contest. And that is a word whose Latin root means to witness or testify. The other runners are witnesses to what he is doing, and therefore, anything else than all he can give is not enough. When you race, you are under oath. When you race, you are testifying as to who you are.

Dr. George Sheehan
Running & Being: The Total Experience
Page 214[1]

With a Blur and a Thunderclap

Mary Lou was beyond words now. All she could do was laugh and shake her fist and laugh some more. There had never been a moment remotely like it in gymnastic history. An American teenager who'd been on her national team for only fourteen months had won the Olympic all-around title by five one-hundredths of a point by nailing her last two routines for perfect scores.

And the way it had ended, with a blur and a thunderclap, brought 9,000 people up out of their seats, mouths agape. Mary Lou was bounding from one end of the building to the other now, propelled by a spontaneous roar of surprise and delight from the stands that began as soon as she touched down and was still reverberating.

It was an American crowd, responding to the kind of moment Americans loved. They were a country of dreamers and gamblers, brought up to believe that anything was possible. If the seventies had made them doubt that, one of their own teenagers had just restored their faith.

Mary Lou had turned fate on its head simply because she believed she could and dared to try. As tribute, an American flag was being readied somewhere in Pauley Pavilion and a gold medal was being unboxed. And still, the cheering went on.

Mary Lou Retton and Bela Karolyi with John Powers
Mary Lou: Creating an Olympic Champion
Pages 158-159[2]

The Fox Trot

I read recently a brief obituary of Terry Fox, dead of cancer at 22. In 1977 his right leg was amputated and he became a thin boy in a wheel chair. His former basketball coach showed him an article about a one-legged man in the New York Marathon, and Terry began to build his body and perfect the strike that came to be called the Fox Trot. On April 12, 1980, Terry began his Canadian "marathon of hope," a coast-to-coast run on an artificial leg to publicize the fight against cancer and raise money for research. Four and a half million and 3,317 miles later, with $24 million raised, he had to stop. The cancer had spread to his lungs, he was hospitalized, pneumonia set in, and Terry Fox died — a deathless symbol to Canada and the world, of courage and of hope. "I wanted to show people that just because they're disabled, it's not the end."

Walter J. Burghardt, S. J.
Seasons That Laugh or Weep
Pages 40-41[3]

Going over the Obvious

Have you ever watched a baseball game and noticed that when a runner gets to first base he has a chat with the first-base coach? I cannot tell you verbatim what is being said, and probably could not get it printed even if I knew. But I know the gist. I can guarantee you that the coach is not trying to come up with something the runner has never heard before. Novelty is irrelevant. The coach is not trying to look insightful or intelligent. His job is to go over the obvious. Make sure the runner is aware of what he ought to have known anyway: how many are out; what to do on certain types of plays that might come up. Good baseball teams communicate with one another, going over the obvious facts, making sure that everyone is concentrating on the basic issues. We disciples need to learn how to coach first base.

I believe a dramatic revolution would sweep through our congregation if we regularly reminded one another to be more loving, if we systematically kept the reminder before us that Jesus is our Lord and Savior. Unhappily we are often afraid to tell old stories, or share what we think people have already heard, and so we keep quiet. Then, Christians we thought were sure of their faith drift away and we discover too late that we should have been witnessing to them all along. We don't stay Christian by hearing only new and excitingly different ideas. We stay Christian by feeding on the meat and potatoes of faith.

John Galloway
How to Stay Christian
Pages 136-137[4]

Just Say What Happened

One of those tales that sports writers hear early in their career involves a World War I correspondent who had witnessed fierce fighting on the muddy battlefields of France. After many months of reporting the bloody carnage, he returned home and was placed on the sports beat. His first assignment was the Harvard-Yale football game at New Haven. The contest was close that year. Besides, the game was crucial because it was . . . well, it was Harvard and Yale.

After the game, the veteran war correspondent sat in silence in front of the typewriter. He couldn't write a word. A colleague reminded him of his deadline, but the stricken writer could only mumble: "I can't do it; it is too much for me; I can't write the story."

Another story being told these days involves love. Whether it means much to us depends on how we invest ourselves in its telling. Whether staged in pageants, sung in oratorios or read as it was originally written, the narrative can touch us at deep levels.

When seen in its fullness the story is so overwhelming that explaining it seems impossible. But I suspect that someone told that war correspondent sitting in the New Haven press box that all he had to do with the Harvard-Yale game was to put down on paper what happened. And, that is all we can do about Bethlehem — just say what happened, and suggest that the story is worth a personal investment.

James M. Wall
"Investing in the Story is Worth the Risk"
The Christian Century
December 11, 1985
Pages 1139-1140[5]

You are Promise

If you say, "She is grace," you tell others more about a dancer or gymnast than if you say, "She is graceful" or "She has grace." If she *is* grace, she takes on all the properties of gracefulness; you will not know how grace looks or is supposed to look until you watch her in action. Similarly, the phrase, "He *is* courage" tells us that an athlete or a soldier shows all the qualities that go with heroism. These phrases are rarely used because we do not find many people who live up to them.

"You are promise." People should feel free to use this phrase more liberally. In some sense or other, it ought to apply to virtually all humans. I would say *everyone* is promise, but that might be too literal. Does someone who is "hopelessly retarded" or in a coma near death embody or represent promise? On the basis of reports of what severely handicapped and dying people have done to expand the lives of others, it might be wiser to reserve judgment. In the meantime, it seems worthwhile to use the equation sign and say that "to be human = to be promise."

Martin E. Marty
You are Promise
Pages 16, 18[6]

Muscular Christianity
and Radiant Goodness

If you saw the Academy Award-winning film *Chariots of Fire*, you will recall the jolt you felt as you read at the close these words about one of the heroes of the film:

Eric Liddell, missionary,
died in occupied China
at the end of World War II
All of Scotland mourned.

I remember seeing Eric Liddell just the day before he died. For more than two years of our wartime captivity, our school was interned in the same camp as he was. That day he was walking slowly under the trees near the camp hospital beside the open space where he had taught us children to play basketball and rounders. As usual, he had a smile for everyone, especially for us.

The athlete who had refused to run on a Sunday in the 1924 Olympic Games in Paris, but who later won the gold medal and created a world record in the 400-meters, was now — twenty-one years later at the age of forty-three — reaching the tape in his final race on earth. We knew nothing of the pain he was hiding, and he knew nothing of the brain tumor that was to take his life the next evening, February 21, 1945.

I remember being part of the honor guard made up of children from the Chefoo and Weihsien schools. None of us will ever forget this man whose humble life combined muscular Christianity with radiant goodness.

David J. Michell
"I Remember Eric Liddell"
Eric H. Liddell
The Disciplines of the Christian Life
Pages 12-13[7]

Appendix

Athletic Images in the New Testament

Revised Standard Version

1 Corinthians 9:24-27

Do you not know that in a race all the runners compete, but only one receives the prize? So run that you may obtain it. Every athlete exercises self-control in all things. They do it to receive a perishable wreath, but we an imperishable. Well, I do not run aimlessly, I do not box as one beating the air; but I pommel my body and subdue it, lest after preaching to others I myself should be disqualified.

Galatians 2:2, 5:7

I went up by revelation; and I laid before them (but privately before those who were of repute) the gospel which I preach among the Gentiles, lest somehow I should be running or had run in vain.

You were running well; who hindered you from obeying the truth?

Romans 9:16

So it depends not upon man's will or exertion, but upon God's mercy.

Philippians 1:29-30

For it has been granted to you that for the sake of Christ you should not only believe in him but also suffer for his sake, engaged in the same conflict which you saw and now hear to be mine.

Philippians 2:16

Holding fast the word of life, so that in the day of Christ I may be proud that I did not run in vain or labor in vain.

Philippians 3:12-14

Not that I have already obtained this or am already perfect; but I press on to make it my own, because Christ Jesus has made me his own. Brethren, I do not consider that I have made it my own; but one thing I do, forgetting what lies behind and straining forward to what lies ahead, I press on toward the goal for the prize of the upward call of God in Christ Jesus.

Colossians 1:29—2:1

For this I toil, striving with all the energy which he mightily inspires within me. For I want you to know how greatly I strive for you, and for those at Laodicea, and for all who have not seen my face.

1 Timothy 4:7-10

Have nothing to do with godless and silly myths. Train yourself in godliness; for while bodily training is of some value, godliness is of value in every way, as it holds promise for the present life and also for the life to come. The saying is sure and worthy of full acceptance. For to this end we toil and strive, because we have our hope set on the living God, who is the Savior of all men, especially of those who believe.

1 Timothy 6:11-12

But as for you, man of God, shun all this; aim at righteousness, godliness, faith, love, steadfastness, gentleness. Fight the good fight of the faith; take hold of the eternal life to which you were called when you made the good confession in the presence of many witnesses.

2 Timothy 2:5

An athlete is not crowned unless he competes according to the rules.

2 Timothy 4:6-8

For I am already on the point of being sacrificed; the time of my departure has come. I have fought the good fight, I have finished the race, I have kept the faith. Henceforth there is laid up for me the crown of righteousness, which the Lord, the righteous judge, will award me on that Day, and not only to me but also to all who have loved his appearing.

Hebrews 12:1-2

Therefore, since we are surrounded by so great a cloud of witnesses, let us also lay aside every weight, and sin which clings so closely, and let us run with perseverance the race that is set before us, looking to Jesus the pioneer and perfecter of the faith, who for the joy that was set before him endured the cross, despising the shame, and is seated at the right hand of the throne of God.

Hebrews 12:11

For the moment all discipline seems painful rather than pleasant; later it yields the peaceful fruit of righteousness to those who have been trained by it.

Jude 3

Beloved, being very eager to write to you of our common salvation, I found it necessary to write appealing to you to contend for the faith which was once for all delivered to the saints.

Scripture Index

Notes and Acknowledgments

Chapter 1: Contending

1. Stephen Brown, *If God Is In Charge* . . .(Nashville, Tennessee: Thomas Nelson Publishers, 1983), p. 138. Used by permission of Thomas Nelson Publishers.

2. Louis H. Evans, Jr., *Hebrews, The Communicator's Commentary* (Waco, Texas: Word Books, Publisher, 1985), p. 218. Copyright 1985, Word Inc., Dallas, Texas. Used by permission.

3. Howard Thurman, *Disciplines of the Spirit* (Richmond, Indiana, United Press, First Edition, 1977, Second Edition, 1987), p. 31.

4. Louis H. Evans, *Make Your Faith Work* (Westwood, New Jersey: Fleming H. Revell Company, 1957), pp. 40-41.

5. Excerpted from Leslie Bush, "A Diving Lesson," *New Catholic World,* March-April, 1985, p. 77. Used by permission of Paulist Press.

6. John Wooden, as told to Jack Tobin, *They Call Me Coach* (Waco, Texas: Word Books, Publisher, 1972). p. 136.

7. Robert K. Hudnut, *This People, This Parish* (Grand Rapids, Michigan: Ministry Resources Library, Zondervan Publishing House, 1986), p. 79. Used by permission of Robert K. Hudnut, copyright 1986.

Chapter 2: Training

1. Orien Johnson, *Becoming Transformed* (Valley Forge, Pennsylvania: Judson Press, 1973), p. 73. Used by permission of Judson Press.

2. J. Ellsworth Kalas, *Reading the Signs* (Lima, Ohio: The C.S.S. Publishing Company, Inc., 1988), p. 48.

3. Earl Palmer, *The 24-Hour Christian* (Downers Grove, Illinois: Inter Varsity Press, 1987), p. 88. Used by permission of Inter Varsity Press, P.O. Box 1400, Downers Grove, Illinois 60515.

4. Lance Webb, *On the Edge of the Absurd* (Nashville, Tennessee: Abingdon Press, 1965), p. 94. Copyright 1965 by Abingdon Press. Used by permission.

5. R. Maurice Boyd, *A Lover's Quarrel with the World* (Philadelphia, Pennsylvania: The Westminster Press, 1985), p. 25.

6. James W. Angell, *Accept No Imitations* (Nashville, Tennessee: Abingdon Press, 1984), p. 121. Copyright 1984 by Abingdon Press. Used by permission.

7. John Thomas Randolph, *The Best Gift* (Lima, Ohio: The C.S.S. Publishing Company, Inc. 1983), pp. 70-71.

8. Joseph M. Stowell, "The Only Good Fight," *Moody Monthly,* October, 1988 , p. 4. Used by permission of *Moody Monthly.*

Chapter 2: Training (continued)

9. James D. Glasse, *Putting It Together in the Parish* (Nashville, Tennessee, Abingdon Press, 1972), pp. 113, 116. Copyright 1972 by Abingdon Press. Used by permission.

10. Gordon MacDonald, *Rebuilding Your Broken World* (Nashville, Tennessee: Oliver Nelson, A Division of Thomas Nelson Publishers, 1988), pp. 120-121. Used by permission of Thomas Nelson Publishers.

Chapter 3: Risking

1. Barry L. Johnson, *Choosing Hope* (Nashville, Tennessee: Abingdon Press, 1988), pp. 84-85. Copyright 1988 by Abingdon Press. Used by permission.

2. Henry E. Horn, *The Christian in Modern Style* (Philadelphia, Pennsylvania: Fortress Press, 1968), pp. 2-3. Reprinted by permission from *The Christian in Modern Style* by Henry E. Horn, copyright 1963, Fortress Press.

3. Richard M. Cromie, *Sometime Before the Dawn* (Mount Lebanon, Pennsylvania: Southminster Extended Ministries, 1982), p. 27. Used by permission of Richard M. Cromie.

4. James R. Edwards, "Faith as Noun and Verb," *Christianity Today,* August 9, 1985, p. 21. Used by permission of James R. Edwards.

5. From *Jesus Makes the Difference!* by James A. Harnish, p. 100. Copyright 1987 by The Upper Room, 1908 Grand Avenue, P.O. Box 189, Nashville, Tennessee 37202. Used by permission of the publisher.

6. Rick Cleveland, Gannet News Service, "Bizarre Safety Gets Team Into State's Play Offs," The Marietta *Times,* November 10, 1988, p. 1. Used by permission of the Gannet News Service and The Marietta *Times.*

7. James W. Angell, *Accept No Imitations* (Nashville, Tennessee: Abingdon Press, 1984), pp. 126-127. From *Accept No Imitations* by James Angell. Copyright 1984 by Abingdon Press. Used by permission.

Chapter 4: Motivating

1. John Powell, *Fully Human, Fully Alive* (Allen, Texas: Argus Communications, A Division of DLM, Inc., 1976), pp. 17-18. From *Fully Human, Fully Alive* by John Powell, S. J. Copyright 1976 by Tabor Publishing, 25115 Avenue Stanford, Valencia, California 91355. Used with permission.

2. James R. Bjorge, *Living Without Fear* (C.S.S. Publishing Co., Inc., Lima, Ohio 1977), pp. 94-95.

3. James W. Angell, *Learning to Manage Our Fears* (Nashville, Tennessee: Abingdon Press, 1981), p. 14. From *Learning to Manage Our Fears* by James Angell. Copyright 1981 by Abingdon Press. Used by permission.

Chapter 4: Motivating (continued)

4. David Steele, "Personal Record," *The Presbyterian Outlook,* August 22-29, 1988, p. 12. Used by permission of *The Presbyterian Outlook.*

5. Keith Miller, *The Scent of Love* (Waco, Texas: Word Books Publisher, 1983), pp. 86-87.

6. Louis H. Evans Jr., *Hebrews, The Communicator's Commentary* (Waco, Texas: Word Books Publisher, 1985), p. 221. Copyright 1985, Word, Inc., Dallas, Texas. Used by permission.

7. Charles L. Allen, *The Secret of Abundant Living* (Old Tappan, New Jersey: Fleming H. Revell, Spire Books, 1980), p. 48.

8. Alan Loy McGinnis, *Bringing Out the Best in People* (Minneapolis, Minnesota: Augsburg Publishing House, 1985), pp. 97-98. Reprinted by permission from *Bringing Out the Best in People* by Alan Loy McGinnis, copyright 1985, Augsburg Publishing House.

9. Jim Smoke, *Whatever Happened to Ordinary Christians?* (Eugene, Oregon: Harvest House Publications, 1987), pp. 56-57. Copyright 1987 by Harvest House Publishers, Eugene, Oregon 97402.

10. Alan Loy McGinnis, *Bringing Out the Best in People* (Minneapolis, Minnesota: Augsburg Publishing House, 1985), pp. 65-66. Reprinted by permission from *Bringing Out the Best in People* by Alan Loy McGinnis, copyright 1985, Augsburg Publishing House.

Chapter 5: Playing

1. Bruce Larson, *A Call To Holy Living* (Minneapolis, Minnesota: Augsburg Publishing House, 1988), p. 85. Reprinted by permission from *A Call To Holy Living* by Bruce Larson, copyright 1988, Augsburg Publishing House.

2. Carol Frances Jergen, BVM, "The Play's The Thing," *Lutheran Woman Today,* Vol. 2, No. 3, March 1989, pp. 7-8. Used by permission of Carol Frances Jegen, BVM.

3. Orien Johnson, *Becoming Transformed* (Valley Forge, Pennsylvania: Judson Press, 1973), pp. 74-75. Copyright 1973. Used by permission of Judson Press.

4. Eugenia Price, *At Home On St. Simons* (Atlanta, Georgia: Peachtree Publisher Ltd., 1981), p. 62. Copyright 1981. Used by permission of Peachtree Publisher Ltd.

5. John B. Coburn, *Twentiety-Century Spiritual Leters* (Philadelphia, Pennsylvania: The Westminster Press, 1976), pp. 65-66.

6. Andrew Gilman, "The Name of the Game," *Christian Ministry,* July, 1987, pp. 21, 23.

7. Shirl J. Hoffman, "The Sanctification of Sport," *Christianity Today,* April 4, 1986, p. 19.

Chapter 5: Playing (continued)

8. Lori Johnson Rosenkvist, "Playing Works," *Lutheran Woman Today,* Vol. 2, No. 3, 1989, p. 10. Used by permission of Lori Johnson Rosenkvist.

Chapter 6: Persevering

1. Gordon MacDonald, *Rebuilding Your Broken World* (Nashville, Tennessee: Oliver Nelson, A Division of Thomas Nelson Publishers, 1988), p. 221. Used by permission of Thomas Nelson Publishers.

2. Andre Resner Jr., "A Year of Lament," *The Princeton Seminary Bulletin,* Volume IX, Number 2, 1988, p. 162. Used by permission of *The Princeton Seminary Bulletin.*

3. Lloyd John Ogilvie, *Let God Love You* (Waco, Texas: Word Books, Publisher, 1974), p. 110. Copyright 1974, Word Inc., Dallas, Texas. Used by permission.

4. Dale E. Galloway, *Expect A Miracle* (Wheaton, Illinois: Tyndale House Publishers, Inc., 1982), pp. 60-61. Used by permission of Dale E. Galloway.

5. Earl Palmer, *The 24-Hour Christian* (Downers Grove, Illinois: Inter Varsity Press, 1987), pp. 125-126. Copyright 1987 by Earl Palmer. Used by permission of Inter Varsity Press, P.O. Box 1400, Downers Grove, Illinois 60515.

6. John Wooden, as told to Jack Tobin, *They Call Me Coach* (Waco, Texas: Work Books, Publisher, 1972), p. 111.

7. Frank C. Laubach, *Channels of Spiritual Power* (Westwood, New Jersey: Fleming H. Revell Company, 1954), p. 136.

Chapter 7: Projecting

1. William Barclay, *A Spiritual Autobiography* (Grand Rapids, Michigan: William B. Eerdmans Publishing Company, 1975), pp. 3-4. Used by permission of William B. Eerdmans Publishing Company.

2. Roberta Louis Hestenes, "Renewal Amidst the Darkness," *The Power To Make Things New,* edited by Bruce Larson (Waco, Texas: Word Books Publisher, 1986), p. 88. Copyright 1986, Dallas, Texas. Used by permission.

3. Robert C. Shannon, "Let Me Illustrate," *Pulpit Digest,* January-February, 1988, p. 65.

4. Jim Conway, *Men in Mid-life Crisis* (Elgin, Illinois: David C. Cook Publishing Company, 1978), pp. 90-91. Used by permission of David C. Cook Publishing Company, *Men in Mid-Life Crisis* by Jim Conway, copyright 1978.

5. Jim Smoke, *Whatever Happened to Ordinary Christians?* (Eugene, Oregon: Harvest House Publishers, 1987), p. 163, 167, 169. Copyright 1987 by Harvest House Publishers, Eugene, Oregon 97402.

Chapter 7: Projecting (continued)

6. Lloyd John Ogilvie, *Let God Love You* (Waco, Texas: Word Books, Publisher, 1974), p. 112. Copyright 1974, Word Inc., Dallas, Texas. Used by permission.

7. James M. Wall, "A Playing Field for the Boys of Eternity," *Christian Century*, May 17, 1989, p. 515.

Chapter 8: Losing

1. Robert C. Roberts, "The Sanctification of Sport: Competition and Compassion," *Christianity Today,* April 4, 1986, p. 23.

2. Paul Tournier, *The Adventure of Living,* translated by Edwin Hudson (New York, New York: Harper & Row, Publishers, 1965), pp. 99-100.

3. C. W. Bess, "Homiletic Bias," *Pulpit Digest*, March-April, 1988, p. 66.

4. Charles R. Swindoll, *Hand Me Another Brick* (New York, New York: Bantam Books, 1981), p. 93. Copyright 1978 by Charles Swindoll, A Bantam Book published by arrangement with Thomas Nelson Inc. Used by permission.

5. Lloyd J. Ogilvie, *Making Stress Work For You* (Waco, Texas: Word Books, Publisher, 1984), pp. 101-102. Copyright 1984, Word Inc., Dallas, Texas. Used by·permission.

6. Dale E. Galloway, *Expect A Miracle* (Wheaton, Illinois: Tyndale House Publishers, Inc., 1982), p. 109. Used by permission of Dale E. Galloway.

Chapter 9: Winning

1. James W. Angell, *Accept No Imitations* (Nashville, Tennessee: Abingdon Press, 1984), pp. 128-129. Copyright 1984 by Abingdon Press. Used by permission.

2. Howard E. Ferguson, *The Edge* (Fairview Park, Ohio: written and published by Howard E. Ferguson, 1982), p. 2-9. Used by permission of Howard E. Ferguson, *The Edge*, 22445 Lorain Road, Fairview Park, Ohio 44126, phone (216) 734-3233.

3. William Toohey, *Life After Birth: Spirituality For College Students* (New York, New York: The Seabury Press, 1980), pp. 60-61.

4. Richard M. Cromie, *Some Time Before the Dawn* (Mount Lebanon, Pennsylvania: Southminster Extended Ministries, 1982), pp. 68-69. Copyright 1982. Used by permission of Richard M. Cromie.

5. Howard E. Ferguson, *The Edge* (Fairview Park, Ohio: written and published by Howard E. Ferguson, 1982), p. 1-1. Used by permission of Howard E. Ferguson, *The Edge*, 22445 Lorain Road, Fairview Park, Ohio 44126, phone (216) 734-3233.

Chapter 9: Winning

6. Peter Kreeft, *Making Sense of Suffering* (Ann Arbor, Michigan: Servant Books, 1986), pp. 132-133.

7. Tim Cloyd quoted in Betty Shannon Cloyd, *Glory Beyond All Comparison* (Nashville, Tennessee: The Upper Room, 1981), p. 57. Copyright 1981 by the Upper Room, 1908 Grand Avenue, P.O. Box 189, Nashville, Tennessee 37202. Used by permission of the publisher.

8. Jimmy Carter, *Why Not the Best?* (Nashville, Tennessee: Broadman Press, 1975), pp. 36-37. All rights reserved. Used by permission.

9. Roger Prescott, *The Second Mile* (Lima, Ohio: The C.S.S. Publishing Company, Inc., 1985), p. 78.

Chapter 10: Witnessing

1. Dr. George Sheehan, *Running and Being: The Total Experience* (New York, New York: Simon and Schuster, 1978), p. 214. Copyright 1978 by George A. Sheehan, M.D., Reprinted by permission of Simon and Schuster Inc.

2. Mary Lou Retton and Bela Karolyi with John Powers, *Mary Lou: Creating an Olympic Champion* (New York, New York: McGraw-Hill Book Company, 1986), pp. 158-159.

3. Walter J. Burghardt, S. J., *Seasons That Laugh or Weep* (Ramsey, New Jersey: Paulist Press, 1983), pp. 40-41. Copyright 1983 by Walter J. Burghardt, S. J. Used by permission of Paulist Press.

4. John Galloway, *How To Stay Christian* (Valley Forge, Pennsylvania: Judson Press, 1984), pp. 136-137. Used by permission of Judson Press.

5. James M. Wall, "Investing in the Story is Worth the Risk," *The Christian Century*, December 11, 1985, pp. 1139-1140.

6. Martin E. Marty, *You Are Promise* (Allen, Texas: Argus Communications, 1973), pp. 16, 18. Copyright 1973 by Tabor Publishing, 25115 Avenue Stanford, Valencia, California 91355. Used with permission.

7. David J. Michelle, "I remember Eric Liddell," Eric H. Liddell, *The Disciplines of the Christian Life* (Nashville, Tennessee: Abingdon Press, 1985), pp. 12-13, 18. Copyright 1985 by the Estate of Florence Liddell Hall. Used by permission of the publisher, Abingdon Press.